"MUTABARUKA IS THE MOST POWERFUL EXPONEI
MUSIC SINCE BOB MARLEY."

Los Angeles Times

"Mutabaruka presents profound ideas in an uncomplicated way, adding a strong pinch of humour to get the lesson across more effectively."

The Jamaica Daily Gleaner

"Back in the mid-'80s, when guntalk and slackness turned the dancehall into a cesspool, a new crop of reggae vocalists emerged to (briefly) wrestle the mike away from the don dadas and bring reggae back to its roots. Calling themselves 'dub poets,' artists such as Jamaica's Oku Onuora and Britain's Linton Kwesi Johnson combined the deejay's spoken word acrobatics with live backing bands to breathe fresh life into conscious reggae. One of the most memorable artists to emerge from this movement was Mutabaruka, who combined classic Rasta themes with proletarian polemics on such classics as 'De System' and 'Dis Poem'."

CD Now

"Mutabaruka is Reggae's premier dub poet."

Billboard

"Mutabaruka's dreadlocks have a white stripe through the top, enhancing the intimidating presence of a man whose spiritual and political poetry flows over solemn, righteous reggae tracks that immediately demand your attention and refuse to let go."

Rolling Stone

"Jamaican dub poet Mutabaruka recalls the aesthetics of invocation."

African-American Review

"Mutabaruka is a dub poet who combines social commentary with scathing personal analysis and endearing humour."

The B.B.C.

"Dub Poet, radio host, and author, Mutabaruka is Jamaica's voice of the people... known for his rhythmic delivery of cutting edged no nonsense commentary on politics, oppression, and human rights ...he is the quintessential poet blending thought provoking lyrics and Reggae rhythms mesmerizing people all over the world."

World Music Central

mutabaruka:
the next poems

(1980-2002)

with an introduction by
Mervyn Morris

A PAUL ISSA PUBLICATION

MUTABARUKA: THE NEXT POEMS / THE FIRST POEMS

Paul Issa Publications
53 South Camp Road
Kingston 4, Jamaica
Telephone: (876) 938-4391
Email: paulissa@cwjamaica.com

ISBN 976-610-713-0
08 07 06 05   5 4 3 2

SECOND PRINTING

MUTABARUKA: THE NEXT POEMS (1980–2002)
© 2005 by Mutabaruka. All rights reserved.

Creole translation for "Haiti" by Myrtha Desulmé
Cover photograph by Brian Jahn

MUTABARUKA: THE FIRST POEMS (1970–1979)
© 1980 by Mutabaruka. All rights reserved.
Many of these poems were previously published in
Twenty-Four Poems © 1972 by Mutabaruka;
Outcry © 1973 by Mutabaruka; and
Sun and Moon © 1976 by Faybiene Miranda and Mutabaruka.
Grateful acknowledgement is also made to the following publications
in which some of these poems first appeared: Swing Magazine, Now, and Savacou.
© 1980 Paul Issa Publications, Ltd.
    FIRST PRINTING: December, 1980
    SECOND PRINTING: August, 1981
    THIRD PRINTING: June, 1983

Cover photograph by Michael Connelly

Book design, cover and typesetting by Annika Lewinson-Morgan,
        A.C.L. Art & Desktop Services
Cover concept by Paul Issa

Printed in USA

to the energy that is feminine
to mothers sisters daughters wives sweethearts
to the energy that is life

FOREWORD

Since *Mutabaruka: the First Poems* was published in 1980, Mutabaruka has had a remarkable career as a leading proponent of an art form that came into existence at that time – dub poetry, or poetry spoken over reggae rhythms or dubs. Since then, performing and recording poems, rather than publishing them in book form, has been Muta's focus.

But just like his earlier poems, his poems of the last twenty years or so have a strength and rhythm in print – perhaps different to when experienced in performance, but just as powerful.

Mutabaruka: the Next Poems is a collection of work from the period between 1980 and 2002, performed and recorded during that time, but published here on the printed page for the first time.

As a special bonus we have reprinted *Mutabaruka: the First Poems* at the back of this book, giving the reader over three decades' worth of the best of the poet's work.

> *Paul Issa*
> *Kingston, 2005*

INTRODUCTION

by Mervyn Morris

"My poems," Mutabaruka has said, "are to show you the problems that face us in the world and then motivate you to find solutions to these problems – I don't think I could show people how to get out of their problems with poems, but at least I could motivate actions."

> I write a poem
> And feel
> That my poem can create
> Can awaken
> Change

The central concern of Muta, a Rastafarian, is black history/ consciousness/identity/liberation. Though he has also written love poems, poems in defence of the environment, and some acknowledging the role reception plays ("dis poem is to be continued in your mind in your mind/ in your mind in your mind…"), the protest element predominates in Muta's work: protest against poverty, inequality, racism, class prejudice ("i am de man/ you love to hate"), oppression, cowardice, political deceit and the wickedness of powerful nations. Most often he tackles the Caribbean and the USA but he will also identify the enemy in Africa, Latin America, Europe, anywhere – "the world needs re-arrangin".

Socio-economic deprivation is often seen to stem from imperialism, neocolonialism, and the mis-education of blacks ("everything we know is wrong"). He is on "the quest to know when where and why/ the quest to seperate truth from lie"; and, ultimately, he is optimistic:

> the mystery is there you can see
> the truth lives within you and me

For Muta, who performs his poems with or without musical accompaniment, poetry is only one of several instruments for doing the work he has chosen. He is much more than a well-known international recording artist. He owns and operates a sound system that plays black music from all over the world; he conducts a late-night radio talk show; and, in accepting invitations to talk and to read his poems, he seems equally at home in an ordinary classroom and on stage at a reggae concert. When he is on tour he may be addressing college audiences, or mesmerizing huge rock festivals, or playing in small nightclubs. He is an experienced communicator, with charisma and a range of skills.

In a typical performance he does not merely read or recite a set of poems. He talks towards the poems, around the poems, sometimes even instead of the poems. A Muta "reading" is often also a "reasoning".

"I can never tell," he says, "what going go in me mind." And: "I find that sometimes when I'm speaking the audience gets so involved with the rapping that I continue it." Normally, when poets appear on stage, their poems – introduced briefly or at greater length – are the central focus. Muta most often presents the philosophy and opinions of Mutabaruka; his poems are only part of the flow.

The poems, composed for oral delivery, usually rhyme and are rhythmically emphatic. They frequently employ rhetorical repetition, as in "Letter from a Friend" ("no martyrs are among you"), "Thievin Legacy" ("gimme mi dis/ gimme mi dat/ gimme back mi everyting yu got"), or "The Eyes of Liberty":

> u invade grenada
> u invade nicaragua
> u bomb hiroshima
> u bomb philadelphia

The rap is usually laced with humour. The poems are presented more solemnly, though they include the occasional pun (as in "strawberry ice cream/ rasberry ice cream/ dem a bury wi/ u nuh si") or laughter-inducing surprise (as at the end of "I Am De Man"). "Dis Poem", playfully self-reflexive, "is watchin u/ tryin to make sense from dis poem", but it also evokes black history, with allusions to ancient and modern achievement, oppression, slavery and heroic rebellion.

Paul Issa published a book by Muta nearly twenty-five years ago; and many of the Muta CDs since then have included texts. Although there is no substitute for Muta in performance, it is good to have this fuller collection of Mutabaruka poems.

Kingston, 2005

MERVYN MORRIS, now Professor Emeritus, retired from the University of the West Indies in 2002. His books of poetry include *The Pond*, *Shadowboxing*, *Examination Centre* (New Beacon Books) and *On Holy Week* (Dangaroo Press). He is the author of '*Is English We Speaking*' *and Other Essays* (Ian Randle Publishers).

The Poems

The 1980s

A Voice 1
Butta Pan Kulcha 2
My Great Shun 4
Old Cut Bruk 6
Bun Dung Babylon 8
Dis Poem 10
Famine Injection 12
The Eyes of Liberty 14
Walkin on Gravel 16
H2 Worka 18
Revolt Aint a Revolution 20
Letter from a Friend 22
Big Mountain 24
Thievin Legacy 26
Miss Lou 28
Would U 30
Sit Dung pon de Wall 33

The 1990s

I Am de Man 34
Wind of Time 36
Ecology Poem 38
Junk Food 40
I Don't Have a Colour Problem 42
Killin 44
Columbus' Ghost 46
Haiti 49
Melanin Man 52

The 2000s

Mother Divine 54
Pele 56
Life and Debt 58
War a Gwaan Dung Deh 60
I Write a Poem 61

A Voice

I am just a voice
listen carefully
and you will hear
yourself....

Butta Pan Kulcha

a me one jus a travel de lan
wid mi likkle butta pan
dem nuh andastan
a me one jus a travel de lan
wid mi likkle dutty pan
dem nuh andastan
mi nuh ave nuh fren inna society
mi still a search fi me identity
mi walk dung town
an everyone frown
a jus me one jus a travel de lan
wid mi likkle butta pan
dem nuh andastan
mi walk de lane
in a sun an rain
mi nuh feel nuh pain
mi nuh ave nuh shame
a jus me one jus a travel de lan
wid mi likkle butta pan
dem nuh andastan
mi family lef fi heaven last year
an society seh dem nuh care
dem seh mi mad
mi feel bad
mi nuh ave nuh fren
nuh money fi spen
a jus me one wid me likkle butta pan
dem nuh andastan
mi cook inna it
an mi tek it mek pit
mi nuh ave nuh bed
fi lay mi ead
a me one jus a travel de lan
wid mi likkle butta pan
dem nuh andastan

an society seh
dem nuh care
or maybe is true dem doh aware
dat a man like me
still tryin to be free
from dis misery
dem pass mi pon de street
an hiss dem teeth
but mi laugh inna mi mind
cause a nuh me a commit all de crimes
but is jus time an dem wi si
dat is not me create dis society
an mek it stink
a me one jus a travel de lan
wid mi likkle butta pan
dem nuh andastan

My Great Shun

So yu jus fine out bout
de reality ova deh
lef yard seh... yu wah run weh
now yu a bawl... yu wah come back
betta come quick before de door dem lack

but yu passport nuh up to date
so yu affi wait
si yu grab de bait
si yu grab de bait
dis a de dream yu wanted to wear
now it tun inna nitemare
dere in de slums yu sit an a wanda
if de news is true or is jus propaganda
wid yu jamaican body an yu foreign mind
standin in de welfare line
tryin to get everyting yu can get
neva know yu coulda cold an sweat

but yu lef tinkin yu woulda betta deh
but tings nuh betta... betta weh?
yu visa expire
yu affi tun liar
yu so bold
sweatin in de cold
you are so bold sweatin in the cold

bet yu neva know tings was like dis
in de lan of opportunity an bliss
bet yu neva know seh
sufferation deh everyweh

now yu tink of de lan yu lef behind
quicksan pullin yu caught in de grime
in de lan of opportunity an bliss
doin funny tings jus to exist
tryin to get a piece of de pie
livin in their illusion an lie

yu so bold
sweatin in de cold
you are so bold sweatin in the cold

Old Cut Bruk

great britain great britain
yu can si
dat yu domination is history
yu greatness cease
yu colonies decrease
de seed yu sow get rotten
now yu affi start use dem baton
inna landan
inna birminam
inna brixton
yu subjects nah tek nuh more
dis yah cut nuh ave nuh cure fi sure
dem a guh bruk dung yu door

de soun gawn out
riots all about
now yu subjects time as come
no more slaves in de sun
yu open old cut
now de cut bus
a nuh blood a run... a pus

her majestys subjects on de rampage
dem bruk out a dem cage
now yu cyaa hide
dem already inside

now yu call fi peace an calm
but is all a it de yout dem want
yu open old cut
now de cut bus
a nuh blood a run... a pus

prime ministers beware
yu subjects nuh care
jolly old inglan inna mess
bobby on bicycles put to de test
how many youts yu tink yu can arrest

inna landan
inna birminam
inna brixton
tings get rough
youts nah bluff
betta get some more hancuff

two decade is a very long time
banana boat on de decline
yu cup of tea is gettin cold
yu greatness is growin old
no more stories to be told

yes de yout dem come of age
now dem turnin a new page
yu open old cut
now de cut bus
a nuh blood a run... a pus

big man bolt yu door
youts inna inglan a guh riot some more

Bun Dung Babylon

yu tink a suh it a guh guh all de while
yu use wi every day
an tell wi fi pray
an tings wi get well
but wi still inna hell

wi a guh bun dung babylon

yu tink a suh it a guh guh all de while
year afta year
wi live inna fear
de yout dem cyaa get nuh wuck
dem a tun to garbage truck
while yu buil up yu mansion
an ave wi pon plantation
but mi a fiel slave
mi nuh know how fi behave

wi a guh bun dung babylon

yu tink a suh it a guh guh all de while
yu gi de yout dope
while yu pray to de pope
fi gi yu more time
fi commit more crime
but de same yout yu dope
a guh tek it fi joke
an start a flame
not even yu can tame

im a guh bun dung babylon

yu tink a suh it a guh guh all de while
dat wi a guh run
everytime yu point yu gun
an shoot one a wi
carelessly
one a dem nite
wen yu tink tings ahrite
wen yu a get yu desire
yu house a guh ketch a fire

wi a guh bun dung babylon

well wi nuh tink a suh it a guh guh all de while
yout a guh rise
an realize
dat de time is now
babylon mus bow
tings mus tun
fire mus bun
our freedom mus come

wi a guh bun dung babylon

Dis Poem

dis poem
shall speak of the wretched sea
that washed ships to these shores
of mothers cryin for their young
swallowed up by the sea
dis poem shall say nothin new
dis poem shall speak of time
time unlimited time undefined
dis poem shall call names
names like lumumba kenyatta nkrumah
hannibal akhnaton malcolm garvey
haile selassie
dis poem is vexed about apartheid racism fascism
the klu klux klan riots in brixton atlanta
jim jones
dis poem is revoltin against
1st world 2nd world
3rd world division man made decision
dis poem is like all the rest
dis poem will not be amongst great literary works
will not be recited by poetry enthusiasts
will not be quoted by politicians nor men of religion
dis poem is knives bombs guns blood fire
blazin for freedom
yes dis poem is a drum
ashanti mau mau ibo yoruba nyahbingi warriors
uhuru uhuru
uhuru namibia
uhuru soweto
uhuru afrika
dis poem will not change things
dis poem need to be changed
dis poem is a rebirth of a people
arisin awakin understandin
dis poem speaks is speakin has spoken

dis poem shall continue even when poets
          have stopped writin
dis poem shall survive u me it shall linger in history
in your mind
in time forever
dis poem is time only time will tell
dis poem is still not written
dis poem has no poet
dis poem is just a part of the story
his-story her-story our-story the story still untold
dis poem is now ringin talkin irritatin
makin u want to stop it
but dis poem will not stop
dis poem is long cannot be short
dis poem cannot be tamed cannot be blamed
the story is still not told about dis poem
dis poem is old new
dis poem was copied from the bible your prayer book
playboy magazine the ny times readers digest
the cia files the kgb files
dis poem is no secret
dis poem shall be called boring stupid senseless
dis poem is watchin u tryin to make sense from dis poem
dis poem is messin up your brains
makin u want to stop listenin to dis poem
but u shall not stop listenin to dis poem
u need to know what will be said next in dis poem
dis poem shall disappoint u
because
dis poem is to be continued in your mind in your mind
in your mind in your mind

Famine Injection

is a plan a plan
is a plan yes a plan
destroyin wi lan
wid dem radio active reaction

atmospheric disturbance everywhere
3rd world yu betta beware
radio activity on de lan
killin us by de million
now de weak mus get strong
to de longest livva de earth belong

is a plan a plan
is a plan yes a plan
destroyin wi lan
wid dem radio active reaction

growin food fi sell to dem
wat about our children
industalizin your piece of earth
what dat really worth
dams buil up everywhere
yu nuh si dem nuh care
beware beware

is a plan a plan
is a plan yes a plan
destroyin wi lan
wid dem radio active reaction

divide an rule is de game
act of god dem seh fi blame
but yu nuh si
is only wi
a feel de drought
nuh food a wi mout
wi sell to dem
an buy it back agen

a terrible cycle wi inna mi fren
but call mi mad
is not an act of god

is a plan a plan
is a plan yes a plan
destroyin wi lan
wid dem radio active reaction

star wars is a reality
weather mishaps in de galaxy
temperatures of minus degrees
now everyting mus freeze
food aid is de cry
while they sit an misuse de sky
wake up now men of high

is a plan a plan
is a plan yes a plan
destroyin wi lan
wid dem radio active reaction

The Eyes of Liberty

on that bridge i look and see
the symbol of your justice and equality
standing tall with her torch of flames
now i ask what are your aims

u invade grenada
u invade nicaragua
u bomb hiroshima
u bomb philadelphia

but the eyes of liberty are watching u
to see what next u will do
the eyes of liberty are watching u
your liberty and justice are only for a few
the true owners of your nation
are forced to live on a reservation
now i see u in my land
makin all kinds of plans
spending billions of dollars every year
to keep us all living in fear
economical pressure is your game
liberty reaching with her torch of flames

yes the eyes of liberty are watching u
to yourself u must be true
the eyes of justice are crying out
what is your democracy all about
talk of invading libya
no talk of invading south afrika
but u invade the sandinista government
using jamaica as your caribbean investment
and the palestinians are your biggest resentment
terrorism is the order of the day
where will the children play

u invade grenada
u invade nicaragua
u bomb hiroshima
u bomb philadelphia

the symbol of true justice and equality
stands erect for all to see
making plans for the haitians
helping to keep down the black americans

but the eyes of liberty are watching u
watching all the things u do
the eyes of liberty are watching u
to yourself u must be true

Walkin on Gravel

walkin on gravel in this time
tryin to separate this confusion and crime
ideologies philosophies tryin to save my day
walkin on gravel things stay same way

so i take a trip to a foreign lan
hopin they might have a plan
they had a plan
no solution
more confusion

they were walkin on gravel just like me
everyone tryin to be free

lookin on the childhood i once knew
wonderin why my dreams never came true
thinkin on the good things when i die
tryin to get my piece of the pie
but i was

walkin on gravel in those times
politicians and priests commitin more crimes

so i walk the road hopin to find
what is this confusion in my time
the quest to know when where and why
the quest to separate truth from lie
frustration disillusions cover my track
but this is no time for turnin back
with my bare feet on the ground
walkin on gravel i know where i am bound

so i take a look
what do i see
rich and poor in agony
waitin on that judgment day
hopin there will be a delay

walkin on gravel the road is long
walkin walkin you have to be strong

so i walk the road round and around
always returnin to the same ground
three hundred and sixty degrees if you please
the road had neither start nor end
neither points not even a bend
so i stopped to look
in the great book
now you may ask
what did i see
but it was the solution to this mystery
after goin round and around all this time
i found that the confusion was in my mind
this mystery is there you can see
the truth lives within you and me

H2 Worka

i am a H2 worka
comin from de island of jamaica
i am a H2 worka
cuttin cane inna florida
workin suh hard in de burnin sun
wonderin if slavery really dun
i'm workin... workin
workin on yu cane field still
workin workin
workin for yu meager dolla bill
suh dont bite de hands dat feed yu
i have dreams like yu to
dont treat mi like i'm a slave here
jus gimme a wage dat is fair

i am a H2 worka
pickin apple inna florida
i am a H2 worka
hopin dat tings will be betta
suh dont tek mi fi granted and pass mi
like is only yu cane and apple yu si
dont tek it fi joke an run mi
den sen to mi govament fi more a wi
dis is not slavery
jus poverty
talkin to democracy

betta yu did sen mi to war
den a woulda si what a fightin for
jus de needy
talkin to de greedy
jus de goodness
of de restless
wantin to make a betta life
for mi children and wife

suh a come to yu lan to help yu
to help mi
to help wi
dis is not slavery
jus poverty
wantin democracy

suh dont bite de hands dat feed yu
i have dreams like yu to
dont tek mi situation fi weakness
dont even tink dat i am helpless
...a gettin restless...
workin on yu cane field still

i'm workin workin
workin on yu cane field still

Revolt Aint a Revolution

why are we fightin each other
tryin to overthrow our brother
why are we still sayin freedom
still freedom cant come
we have to learn things from ancient history
to help build a new society
we have to remember nkrumah and garvey
to build our own economy

now a revolt aint a revolution
coup is still not the solution
we have to plant some food on the land
agriculture is the key for buildin a nation

why are we measurin progress
as determined by the west
why are we still sayin yes
to all their industrial mess
we have to understan the times we are livin in
and remember where we have been
we have to remember what happened in slavery
so as not to repeat that history

now a revolt aint a revolution
killin leaders is not the solution
we have to build schools in the community
to get rid of illiteracy

why are we listening to these preachers
who pose as moral teachers
why are we still sayin amen
to the very thing that put us in this pen
we have to return to ancient philosophy
and reveal all of earths mystery
we have to live by our own spirituality
to determine our own destiny

now a revolt aint a revolution
foreign aid is still not the solution
we have to understan afrika for afrikans
to build a new nation

why are we discussin problems
with people who refuse to solve them
why are we still beggin for freedom
while lookin down the barrel of a gun
we have to seek shaka hannibal
in these times of aggression
and understan what was their mission
we have to advance to victory with truth and right
known that right must overcome might

now a revolt aint a revolution
buildin nuclear weapons is not the solution
if some thing is not worth dyin for
its not worth livin for
but if it takes war to free us
then is just WAR....

Letter from a Friend

from where i stand
i can clearly see your tormented faces
how you must hate me
i wonder how many think of killing me
of assassinating their country's leader
but again looking at you all
i see fear
passive fear
fear of death
no martyrs are among you

so i am safe within the confines of the law
to overtax you
underpay you
overwork you
police force you
bury you
black people
my people
victims of society
victims of western democracy
no martyrs are among you

even though our country achieved independence
european rule still prevails
neo-colonialism has its roots deep in our soil
i care not
as long as i am well paid
no martyrs are among you

so i am safe within the confines of your passivity
to stand at this rostrum
and address you
and fill your oppressed ears
with mocking promises

as i speak, i speak for all who are here with me
brown and nearly white
for color, class and creed
have no meaning where the almighty dollar is
concerned
and on behalf of the government
here and abroad
i would like to thank you voters
for dipping your finger in the blood
thus marking an X
giving us the wrong to do wrong
you don't have to hear my thoughts
you know them
no martyrs are among you

Big Mountain

REDMAN REDMAN
YU AFFI FIGHT FI YU LAN
JUS LIKE DE DAYS OF OLD
YU WILL AFFI BE COLD AND BOLD

dont let de witeman tongue fool yu
dont let his paper cool yu
with tricks and lies he stole de land
refuse and resist de witeman plan
stand on big mountain its your ancestors earth
land is power without it life has no worth
stand on big mountain you'll have to be strong
good must overcome the struggle is long

he came to turtle island with fire water in hand
gave it to the redman
then stole his land
gave us a image of indians so wild
de image we got on the screen as a child
who is to blame who is to blame
i say de image of john wayne

dont let di witeman tongue fool yu
dont let his paper cool yu
dont let his fire water get u down
stand up and fight for your piece of ground
stand on big mountain its your ancestors earth
land is power without it life has no worth
stand on big mountain you'll have to be strong
good must overcome the struggle is long

in afrika and asia he went to civilize nations
yet in the land of liberty and justice he has reservations
on the big screen he played his silly game
usin the image of john wayne
robbin and rapin he stole the land
refuse and resist the witeman plan

dont let the witeman tongue fool yu
dont let his papers cool yu
dont let the ancestors die in vain
yu have nothin to lose much to gain
stand on big mountain its your ancestors earth
land is power without it life has no worth
stand on big mountain you'll have to be strong
good must overcome the struggle is long

Thievin Legacy

gimme mi dis
gimme mi dat
gimme back mi every ting yu got
gimme mi philasophy yu carry to greece
tief homer and socrates
gimme back mi historical masta piece
gimme back mi name
gimme mi back mi kalinda
gimme mi books yu tief from alexandria
gimme mi queen like kleopatra
mi nuh wah ear bout queen victoria
gimme mi language a know suh well
yu mixup inglish confusin nuh hell
gimme back mi maths yu pythagoras
gimme mi symbols yu tief from us

gimme mi dis
gimme mi dat
gimme back mi every ting yu got
gimme mi diamon
gimme mi gold
gimme back mi rack and roll
gimme mi uranium
gimme mi coal
gimme mi reggae
gimme mi blues
gimme mi musik dat yu confuse

no spiritual concept originated here
suh who i praise yu shouldnt care
yu seh steal not
yu tief mi lan
sex not
yu rape mi mada
keep de sabbat
wi work seven days a week

yu buil a nation from de sweat off mi back
now yu wah come gimme CRACK?

gimme mi herbs mek wi mek some tea
gimme back all mi fruit tree
gimme mi medicin yu tek from mi
gimme de remidy dat mek bline see

gimme mi dis
gimme mi dat
gimme back mi every ting yu got
gimme a space a can run mi own life
respect is due de time is now
no more tun cheek
dis time wi nah bow

                              gimme a break....

Miss Lou

Miss Lou Miss Lou
wi love yu fi true
wi love how yu chat
some nuh love dat
Miss Lou

Miss Lou Miss Lou
yu heavy fi true
mi seh wi love weh yu seh
when yu seh weh yu seh
Miss Lou

a years now wi si
weh yu do fi poetry
here in jamaica
usin our patwa
mi know nanny a hero fi true
but mi tink yu a hero too
mi watch de children a dance an sing
an yu teach dem how fi play ring ding
Miss Lou

Miss Lou yu mek dem know
dat is from de base tings jamaica grow
dem use fi seh wi mus speak in twang
but yu mek wi proud seh wi a afrikan
now wi si dem a teach in school
dat jamaica patwa is not fi fool
when yu chat it soun suh sweet
an all a jamaica jus a skin dem teeth
Miss Lou

mutabaruka

Miss Lou Miss Lou
wi love yu fi true
wi love how yu chat
some nuh love dat
Miss Lou

Miss Lou Miss Lou
yu heavy fi true
mi seh wi love weh yu seh
when yu seh weh yu seh
Miss Lou

Would U

when i speak
do u feel weak
when u hear my thoughts
do u feel caught in the web of hopelessness

when i say black
do u feel its an attack
or a lack of understandin on my part
or just wrath
comin from me
do u see
me
as a threat to your safety
when i say whitey
do u consider that bigotry
if i say i cared not about politics
would u consider me an anarchist
if i say no to religion
would that be an extention
of my misconcepton
about what u think of me
do u see what i mean

if i said i didnt smoke
or take coke
would u take it for a joke
and cry then wonder why i told such a lie
are u upset because my poems sometimes make u fret
about the future of things to come

would u call me a brute
if i wore a suit
or said i was cute
do u think i would be a better writer
if my poems were lighter
spoke more about nature
or some adventure
that gave me pleasure

would u love me more
if i spoke less about the poor
and talked about the women i adore

now after listenin to this
are u lookin for a twist
or just another rhyme
in the next line

the solutions that u seek
will not be in the streak
of a pen or even ten lines
of mine

the problems are the same
but dont blame me because i see
that part of reality
that pains
and stains the heart
i came into this life
with neither guns nor knives
i made no laws
with all their flaws
about black and white
and whats wrong from whats right
i speak i write of what i see
of men holdin men in slavery
of colour class and greed

so dont blame me if when i speak
u do feel weak
i did not create hate

tell me this now
would u accuse me of causin a riot
if i was
quiet
would u

Sit Dung pon de Wall

a sit dung pon de wall
a watch im a watch mi
is lang lang time
a sit dung pon de wall
a watch im a watch mi
im pants match im shirt
not even im shoes look like it eva touch dirt
suh a sit dung pon de wall a watch im a watch mi
is lang lang time
a sit dung pon de wall a watch im a watch mi
9 to 5 to stay alive
im a eat... im a bawl
im a sleep... im a bawl
im a... im a bawl
an dats not all
still sit dung pon de wall a watch im a watch mi
im check seh me fool
i well well cool
suh dis marnin im pass
im neva si mi
im look north
im look south
a could si im was in doubt
but a was sittin down in de street
pickin last week food from out a mi teeth
im neva andastan
seh a neva ave nuh plan
suh im start fi run
an a car lick im dung
man
is lang lang time
a sit dung pon de wall
a watch im a watch mi

I Am de Man

i am de man
you love to hate
sitting in the slums of
ghost town
trench town
back o' wall
no clothes
to hide my nakedness
filth and mosquitoes smelling
biting 400 years of black flesh
scarred by whips and sticks
i am de man
locks entangled in
your nightmares of
medusas and gorgons
unkept religious beliefs
that pierce the side of
your jesus in the sky
your vinegar has turned to blood
your water to mud
crucifix
choking on your life
of neo-colonialistic attitudes
yes i am de man
that came in
clouds of ganja smoke
choking you to death
yet
not killing you
my eyes
seeing a black god
casting doubt in your
mind about your
unexposed spiritual being

black shadows
casting clear pictures
of an existence
drowned by
false concepts of reality
black was beauty
until i walked
with my barefeet
touching your
tarry pavements of
sadistic heat

u would have accepted i
if i came via
time magazine
or
vogue
if only you were exposed
to life
beyond your
middle class gate
i am de man
you love to hate
look
I am now your
next door neighbour

Wind of Time

i hear the sound of the wind
rushin to the sea
i hear the wind callin
who will come with me
the tides are a changin
the world needs re-arrangin
who will come with me
in the depths of the earth
breathes life forever
the peace that men desire
is burnin in the heart of the fire
so who's gonna take the blame
who's gonna end the game

in the wind i hear 10,000 voices
beckonin for freedom
in the wind i see hands reachin
come... come... come...
quick give me your hand
let us walk on the sand
before the sea comes in… and
takes away the land

everything must change they say
the voice of the wind is fading away
now time and only time will tell
if there is a heaven or a hell
i watched the sea rushin into shore
trying to take the footprints
to the ocean floor
the tides came in
but the prints were blown away by the wind

now i hear the wind howlin
again
who's gonna take the blame
who's gonna take the blame
who's gonna take the blame
who's gonna end the game

Ecology Poem

now u mixin up fantasy
wid reality
cuttin down de tree
no leaves to stop de smoke
chokin our lives to death
wi fret
an wanda why
people die
de earth breathes
an no one feels
cant u see
we
are usin up our time
its a crime
down right insanity
mixin up fantasy
not knowin reality
ozone depletion
no discretion
soon mutation
man pollution
man destruction
when will we see
that fantasy is not reality
disregardin health
storin up wealth
is dis a joke
we might all go up in smoke

take a look at u and me
check what is been done to de sea
fishes cannot breathe on lan
talkin about mutation
de forest
de birds animals too
tell me what are dey supposed to do
when you build your world
of pollution
is total annihilation
your solution
so what are u going to do
to help us get through
dis seeming cloud of gloom
dat could bring mans doom
wake up to this gift around
listen to de sound
of de earth de trees
de sky
den tell me why
must we die
because u cant tell fantasy
from reality
tell me why must we die
usin vanity
trying to save humanity
with your insanity
mixin fantasy
with reality
tell me why

Junk Food

rememba de cold suppa shop
dat u use fi stop at
u coulda eat anythin
it was like u granny cookin
corn dumplin and ackee
from big fat mattie
stew peas and rice
use fi really taste nice
now a ice cream stand
teckin ova de lan

junk food fullin up de place
dis is annada disgrace
junk food fullin up de place
a now good food a guh guh
to waste

u know dat sweet will
rot u teeth
but is only ice cream u a guh
get fi eat
jooks pon de corna a tek in
de scene
puffing up u belly wid ice cream
de scene get mean

junk food fullin up de place
dis is annada disgrace
junk food fullin up de place
a now good food a guh guh
to waste

run u mus
but u belly might buss
gun shot clap
one a u fren drop
flex out time
flex out time
leavin u ice cream behin

junk food fullin up de place
dis is annada disgrace
junk food fullin up de place
a now good food a guh guh
to waste

folla fashion is de order of de day
cyaa get nuh food dat is wat dem seh
miss mattie shop affi move
granny cooking out a groove
de disk jockey seh
announcin de openin of a
ice cream stan
in de parish of St. Ann
nex month is Westmoreland
an annada one in Clarendon
watch out Portland

strawberry ice cream
rasberry ice cream
dem a bury wi
u no si
ice cream ice cream
hot dog ice cream
livin de american dream

I Don't Have a Colour Problem

i doh ave a colour problem
i si everyting in black
wen a walk a nite
i doh si neon lite
an at crismus
nuttin fi mi tun white
i si everyting in black
black dungeons
holdin black bodies
to be sold for a price

i doh ave a colour problem
i come from a black womb
enter a black worl
fill wit black devils
doing everyting
black dat was bad

in de blackess corner of my mind
i created nuttin of colour
my soul filled with devils
sowin seeds of ugliness
black magic castin shadows
of past pains
ugliness prevails black as sin
yet... i entered a black flesh
dat conceived a black child
who was taught on a black slate
by way of a black board
i learnt about the black market
bodies sold on auction blocks
money sold for more than its value

i doh ave a colour problem

bad luck
keep passin my way
by way of a black cat
so i write a letter an black mail it
black listed for speaking
about the dark
continent
my mind like a sponge
absorbin
yet like a mirror
reflectin
the rain clouds have covered the rainbow
i am the black sheep in my family

i doh have a colour problem
i see everyting in black

i rememba dem tell mi
black is not a colour
colour is not black
Nat Cole was black
black make sense
black make no sense
no sense being black
not making sense –

a jus ave a black out....

Killin

mek wi talk
mek wi talk
mek wi talk mek wi talk mek wi talk
mek wi talk bout de killin
de killin dat dem neva mention
killin was their intention

blood suede shoes
hands dipped in blood
blood runnin from flesh
so mek wi talk bout de bottom a de sea
escapin from slavery
millions tryin to be free
preferrin death
yet
no mention
de plantation
fightin for liberation
no mention
cause killin was their intention

dyin at their will
in de name of jesus they kill
still wi deyah
but who care
no mention
cause killin is their intention
de lynchin in de south
wen wi open wi mouth
many did die
fi de few who live

thousands of ethiopians sprayed with poison
mussolini army sanctioned by de pope
still wi cope

south afrika children lay dead
gun shots to their head
famine on de lan
a plan
act of god
dem mussi mad

environmental pollution
created by their so-called solution
aids we all agree
is no mystery
lab test
escape what a mess

ova all de earth
life nuh ave nuh worth
but we survive de crimes
still deyah inna these times
blood suede shoes
hands dipped in blood
blood runnin from flesh
so

mek wi talk
mek wi talk
mek wi talk mek wi talk mek wi talk
mek wi talk bout de killin
de killin dat dem neva mention
killin was their intention

> *everyone remembers their past*
> *building monuments museums*
> *writing books*
> *so that their children's children will never forget*
> *we must all learn from the past*
> *so as not to repeat those things*
> *that have kept us back for over*
> *500 years*

Columbus' Ghost

i am christopher columbus
just call me cris
i am de man who did miss the land
india
i thought i'd discover
that which was never
how clever of me to see the land
beyond
i came to tame
and claim
in the name of spain
i am cris
dont dis
my his-story
i inspired hawkins   livingston
mussolini   botha
bush
i exterminated
perpetuated
hatred
against redmen   yellowmen
with blackmen i make no friend
i attack arawak
cut off their head
wrote instead
that the caribs ate them like bread
i never told you this before
but my chief navigator was a moor
you know the moors
they discovered spain
those blacks who came from the afrikan terrain
the idea that the world was round
i got from these same blacks in some little
spanish town
now you may ask what was blacks doin there

but they ruled us for over 700 years
they made a great mistake then
instead of enslavin us they made us their friend
some survived
stayed alive
fought the invasion
european division
english aggression
the fight between europe and european expansion
i wrote your history for you
did not tell you   true
not all blackmen came as slaves
listen you will know the truth in the waves
that brought the ships
lips lie
to keep intact
oppression of black skin
a sin
a myth
i am cris

the church perch on the opportunity to spread
the religion of the dead
through misconception
the assumption
that this world was new
the wind blew us to save the earth
from beast-like men
friend i am not
blot out the spot
that claim they are men like us
i am christopher columbus
i gave europe power over all the earth
500 years of your blood sweat and tears
now you celebrate
recreate your death
let the glasses touch
with the blood of your fathers and mothers
give a toast

host
my arrival
your dyin my survival

the land is still mine
the pope is still the divine
yes
drink your own blood
call it wine
nothin in the pages of my history
will blot out your misery
you shall celebrate my victory
your children praise me
i am their only history
i am christopher columbus
i died
but you made me live
give me the sea once more
let me discover you again
the stain
my fathers sons rule
fool
you celebrate my coming
i will not go
not from your mind
restore me for all to see
keepers of life
shepherds of my people
lead them to the altar of lies
your ancestors cries will not be heard
word after word
pages of history written
the victims are once more bitten

1492 to you
the beginning of western democracy
1492 to me
the beginning of white supremacy

Haiti

haiti yu goin an no one seem to care
haiti yu goin neighbours beware
de poverty an death that haunts every day
de boat dat leave to de u.s.a.
yu payin payin for de afrikanness yu keep
yu payin payin boukman is not asleep
yu gave us haiti de strength to fight
black people in de caribbean i say unite
break de chains dat keep us apart
haiti suffers because it made a start
haiti haiti yu ave de will
haiti haiti afrika calls yu still
too black too strong you'll ave to pay
blacker dan nite never seein de day
but too black is always de reason for your pain
but your fight for freedom will not be in vain
haiti yu goin an no one seem to care
haiti yu goin neighbours beware
de blood sweat an tears dat shed today
will be a guide for afrika an afrikans along de way

cuba beware
jamaika beware
trinidad beware
grenada beware
caribbean beware beware beware
care no fear care no fear
caribbean beware beware beware
break de chains dat keep us apart
haiti suffers because it made a start
but too black is no reason for pain
de blood for freedom will always stain

haiti haiti you ave de will
haiti haiti afrika calls yu still
caribbean leaders what are yu goin to do
today is haiti   tomorrow is yu
today is haiti   tomorrow is yu

ayiti ou prale men peson pa mele
ayiti ou prale vwazen rete sou pinga nou
lamize ak lanmò kap kouri dèyè nou jodi a
batiman kap pati pou lèzetazini
ouap peye peye pou tét ou rete afrikain
ouap peye peye boukman pap domi
ou ba nou fos pou nou goumen ayiti
neg karayib ini nou
kase chenn kap separe nou
ayiti ape soufri pou tèt li se premye
ayiti ayiti ou gen volonte
ayiti ayiti lafrik ape rele ou toujou
trò nwè trò fò ou gen pou ou peye
pi nwè pase lannuit pa ka jam wè limyè
men trò nwè se toujou rezon pou doule ou
men lit ou pou libete pap anven
ayiti ou prale men peson pa mele
ayiti ou prale vwazen rete sou pinga nou
san syè ak lam n ape kriye jodi a
ap toujou gide lafrik ak afriken

kiba rete sou pinga ou
jamayik rete sou pinga ou
trinidad rete sou pinga ou
grenad rete sou pinga ou
karayib rete sou pinga nou
pa kapon pa kapon
karayib rete sou pinga nou
kase chenn kape separe nou
ayiti ou ape soufri pou tèt ou se premye
men trò noe pa yon rezon pou ou soufri
mak san libete ap toujou rete

ayiti ayiti ou gain volonte
ayiti ayiti lafrik ape rele ou toujou
lidè caraïbes, sa nap fè
jodi a se ayiti   demen se nou menm
jodi a se ayiti   demen se nou menm
jodi a se ayiti   demen se nou menm

Melanin Man

i am de melanin man
a come from de melanin lan
i am de melanin man
look at me an u will understand

i absorb de lite
i am de darkness in your nite
de way i dance u see
is just de melanin in me

de tings i tink an feel
is de tings dey try to steal
but look in de sun and u will see
u cannot destroy de melanin in me

i am de melanin man
look at me an u will understan
i am de melanin man
a come from de melanin lan

i am time an space
i will never be erase
de way i sing u see
is just de melanin in me
wen u look at me an tink
do i remind u of blood or ink
any one you perceive me to be
i am indelible
an its de melanin in me

i am de melanin man
look at me an u will understan
i am de melanin man
a come from de melanin lan

i am de dream u dream
i am de reason u scheme
de compassion dat u see
is because of de melanin in me

now de sun is gettin hotter in de sky
dont ask me de reason why
who will survive who will it be
will it be u or de melanin in me

i am de melanin man
look at me an u will understan
i am de melanin man
a come from de melanin lan

Mother Divine

Oh holy mother divine
It is you that carry the bloodline
Replacing you with the Holy Ghost
Men in their egos oh how they boast
Black woman black till blue
Oh how I adore you
In your many shades I cannot resist
The compassion of your heavenly bliss

Black woman divine of the world
More precious than diamond or pearl
You gave your womb as a sacrifice
Now Blackman praise her and rejoice
Empress Menen did take her seat
Emperor and Empress I kiss your feet

Oh holy mother divine
Shades of black saviour of mankind
Father child and mother I profess
Lay patriarchal thinking to rest
Return to the womb once again
Black woman has suffered enough pain
Awake to your mother this is reality
Liberation from Adam and Eve mentality

Blackman now is the time
To leave his-story behind
Cast away that evil spell
You think you're in heaven but you're really in hell
Mother nature mother earth we confess
Life is like milk from a woman's breast

Oh holy mother divine
Shades of black saviour of mankind
Father child and mother I profess
Lay patriarchal thinking to rest

Black woman giver of life
Mother sister sweetheart wife
It is you that has made the sacrifice
In the womb lies the answer to all suffering and shame
From the womb all humans came
And unless a man is born again
Our misery will be the same

His-story has dealt her a terrible blow
His story a puppet show
Myths and legends have shown us the way
His-story will have to die one day
And unless a man is born again
His misery will be the same

Pele

Tears cannot wash away the memories
Of hours spent on the road
Searching for the next hotel or venue
Tears cannot drown the many times we lost and found
The pain of memories lingers forever
Yet joy awaits
Pele Lanier
We shared so much   years of searching
Finding
The music filled our dreams
We live
You knew me
Like a mother on the road
A woman strong and assertive

Tears cannot wash away memories of poetry
Of music   of tours filled with joy and sorrow
Lost and found
Like a calm breeze I felt safe
No question asked
Tears cannot wash away memories
Tears can only wash the heart that touched the soul
Tears free the mind of pain felt
Of the burden of longing for
Pele Lanier

How yu mean fi leave mi?
Wi neva finish yet!

She made the journey that we all make
Yet hoping to stay forever
Knowing the journey is for a time
We laugh   we cry
Life's strange attributes
We search hoping to find the journey of infinity
Elusive dream at least for now

The journey is made
Never ending never coming to end
It takes all of lifetime to come to this point
The joy   the pain
All together makes life journey meaningful
Meaningless if we give up on life's journey
But who knows   she came   partook   left
Weep not world of the living
We all must take that journey's end

Tears will flow
The only comfort for the disturbed soul
I cry
In my car I cry
I cry
In the studio I cry
In the market I cry
I cry because I know you wont be there when
        I ring your number
When I cant be bothered to speak to
        promoters or news reporters
I cry because of how you love me
How you love my work
My faults
My love
I cry because I know like many others
When they say again your name
You will not answer
Tears will not wash away your memory
Not now   not ever
I will cry me a river
And know that it will flow and keep flowing
Till my soul is cleansed of the pain
Pele Lanier
We will keep on
For you   for me
For the time you spent keeping on for us
May your life works keep touching others
Like the river that becomes the ocean

Life and Debt

Dem an dem economical plan
Still cyaa find a solution
Borrowin money fi lend
World Bank a nuh wi friend
Still cyaa find a solution
Borrowin money fi lend
World Bank a nuh wi friend

Is life and debt
All a wi a fret
Life and debt
Freedom not yet

Farmers get a blow
Foreign food suh an suh
Amerikan farmer get a upper hand
While our farmers goin one by one
Bank crash pay slash news flash
Big bwoy hide im stash
Nuh money nuh job
Borrowin money fi lend

Is life and debt
All a wi a fret
Life and debt
Freedom not yet

Caricom carry gone everyting
Too much importin debt increase
Country deh pon lease
Politicians a fraud
De people draw bad card
Tings nuh cool
Dem teck wi fi fool

Gun shot in de street
Blood pon sheet
Sour nuh sweet

Is life and debt
All a wi a fret
Life and debt
Freedom not yet

But tings affi tun
Or a pure fire bun
Someone will affi pay
Nuh more man out a clay
Nuh more blind faith
Wi need food inna wi plate
Look how long wi a sweat
Too much foreign debt

War a Gwaan Dung Deh

War a gwaan dung deh
Mi naw guh dung deh
War a gwaan dung deh
Mi naw guh dung deh

Politicians gawn dung deh
Mi naw guh dung deh
Preacha man gawn dung deh
Mi naw guh dung deh

Yu nuh si weh a gwaan dung deh
Pure arms house a gwaan dung deh
Yu nuh si nuh solution nuh dung deh
An a mi yu wah guh dung deh

Bankers an drugman dung deh
Mi naw guh dung deh
Taxman gawn dung deh
Mi naw guh dung deh

Yu nuh si weh a gwaan dung deh
Pure death and destruction dung deh
Everybody scared a dung deh
An a mi yu wah guh dung deh

Politicians a sell promise dung deh
Mi naw guh dung deh
Preacha a sell sky pie dung deh
Mi naw guh dung deh

Yu nuh si a pure gyow a sell dung deh
Pure illusion an delusion dung deh
Young an old a dead dung deh
An a mi yu wah guh dung deh

War a gwaan dung deh
Mi naw guh dung deh
War a gwaan dung deh
Mi naw guh dung deh

I Write a Poem

I write a poem
A poem to feel the freedom of time
Time is
Yesterday
Today
Tomorrow

I write a poem
Trying to experience
The source of my being
Waiting for the next revelation
Or inspiration
To write a poem

I write a poem
So I can read
I can hear
What I feel about my poem
The ink flows
My mind spiraling
Through the corridors of time

I write a poem
And feel
That my poem can create
Can awaken
Change

I write a poem
And hope for life's goodness
The poem and poet
Must be one

I write a poem
And smile
Laugh
Cry

I feel
Like... like... like...
I am writing a poem
To feel like I can write a poem

I write a poem
And remind myself of Atlas
Holding up the world
Or maybe Christ
Trying to save the world

I write a poem
Only because
I have a pen
A book
With nothing written
A mind
That wanders in space and time
A life
A feeling
Of love
Of joy
For you
Who would read my poem

I write a poem
So that poetry can be
The poet's weapon of freedom

mutabaruka:
the first poems

(1970-1979)

with an introduction by
Mervyn Morris

A PAUL ISSA PUBLICATION

MUTABARUKA: THE NEXT POEMS / THE FIRST POEMS

Paul Issa Publications
53 South Camp Road
Kingston 4, Jamaica
Telephone: (876) 938-4391
Email: paulissa@cwjamaica.com

ISBN 976-610-713-0
08 07 06 05   5 4 3 2

SECOND PRINTING

MUTABARUKA: THE FIRST POEMS (1970–1979)
© 1980 by Mutabaruka. All rights reserved.
Many of these poems were previously published in
Twenty-Four Poems © 1972 by Mutabaruka;
Outcry © 1973 by Mutabaruka; and
Sun and Moon © 1976 by Faybiene Miranda and Mutabaruka.
Grateful acknowledgement is also made to the following publications
in which some of these poems first appeared: Swing Magazine, Now, and Savacou.
© 1980 Paul Issa Publications, Ltd.
    FIRST PRINTING: December, 1980
    SECOND PRINTING: August, 1981
    THIRD PRINTING: June, 1983

Cover photograph by Michael Connelly

MUTABARUKA: THE NEXT POEMS (1980–2002)
© 2005 by Mutabaruka. All rights reserved.

Creole translation for "Haiti" by Myrtha Desulmé
Cover photograph by Brian Jahn

Book design, cover and typesetting by Annika Lewinson-Morgan,
        A.C.L. Art & Desktop Services
Cover concept by Paul Issa

Printed in USA

*The first part of this book is for
all oppressed black people,
everywhere.*

*The second part is for
all oppressed minds,
everywhere.*

FOREWORD

This book is a collection of selected poems written by Mutabaruka during the decade which is over. Although this information is not necessary to the reader, the poems take on additional interest when seen against the backdrop of Jamaica in the 1970s, and within the context of black consciousness, Rastafari, and other social, metaphysical, ontological awakenings of that period, resulting in the relatively high level of societal awareness and cultural identity of Jamaica at the start of the 1980s.

These poems, spanning ten years, serve also as a kind of chronicle of the writer's individual growth both as poet and as man.

With the exception of a few minor corrections, the poems are reproduced here intact, as they were originally published.

I hope that Muta's words – in print once again – will bring you as much pleasure as they have brought me, over the years, and I envy those of you who are about to encounter them for the first time.

Paul Issa
Kingston, 1980

INTRODUCTION

by Mervyn Morris

Mutabaruka (formerly Allan Hope) was born in Rae Town, Kingston, on 26th December, 1952. After primary education he attended Kingston Technical High School, where he was a student for four years. Trained in electronics, he left his first job after about six months and took employment at the Jamaica Telephone Company Limited. During his time at the telephone company he began to examine Rastafarianism and to find it more meaningful than either the Roman Catholicism of his upbringing or the political radicalism into which he had drifted.

In the late 1960s and early 1970s there was an upsurge of Black Awareness in Jamaica, in the wake of a similar phenomenon in the United States. Muta, then in his late teens, was drawn into that movement. Illicitly, in school he read many "progressive books" including Eldridge Cleaver's *Soul on Ice* and some that were then illegal in Jamaica, such as *The Autobiography of Malcolm X*. Muta saw himself as a young revolutionary. But when he deepened his investigation of Rastafarianism, which he once regarded as essentially passive, he came to find its thinking more radical than that of the non-Rastafarian group with which he had associated. While still employed at the telephone company, he stopped combing his hair, started growing locks, altered his diet, and declared himself Rastafarian. A number of his friends thought he was going mad.

After leaving the telephone company, Muta found life in Kingston increasingly unsatisfactory. He and his family left Kingston in 1974 in search of a more congenial environment. They settled in the hills of Potosi District, St. James, in the house that Muta built. Muta has had periods of close contact with the Negril Beach Village, where he explained to guests certain aspects of Jamaican culture. He has talked

at great length with many foreigners, and found the experience broadening. To Muta now, Rastafarianism is part of a universal quest which may also be pursued by other routes, such as Hinduism or Buddhism or Christianity. He disapproves, however, of institutionalized religion: the priest "has used your mind/ to make love/ with the/ dead".

Of course the poems of Mutabaruka reflect the man and the specific contexts of his experience. Mostly in Part Two of this volume a number of poems express a search for spiritual understanding, spiritual peace, and are critical of whatever might impede that search:

> the man spiritual is above all
> the man thinkin is "me"
> thinkin on the care of my body
> of my worldly possessions
> never stoppin to know
> that all worldly
> things
> must
> go.

A number of the poems, mostly in Part One, insist on anger as a proper response to black suffering and deprivation. Some of the pieces dramatize the horrors of slavery, and exhort the Black man to proudly remember African origins, to break out of the prison of self-hatred. Many of the poems attack what they perceive as the cultural imperialism of Europe; Muta sees the need for a Jamaican originality of language, form and attitude which might subvert the hegemony of the British "greats":

> shakespeare/milton/chaucer
> still drenchin
> the souls of black folks
> tryin to integrate
> in my life   your life.

Muta's was the first well-publicized voice in the new wave of poets growing since the early 1970s. They have developed a living relationship between a poet and a fairly wide audience such as, in Jamaica, only Louise Bennett has achieved before them. Early work by Muta regularly appeared in *Swing*, a monthly that gave fullest coverage to the pop music scene. Introducing *Outcry* (March 1973) John A.L. Golding Jr. wrote:

That his poems in *Sun and Moon* (1976), a volume shared with Faybiene, are quieter is one indication of Muta's particular development.

Like Louise Bennett (and like many of the Black Americans of the sixties whose work they had sampled) the new and popular Jamaican poets write mainly in the unofficial language of the people, feel close to the Black musicians (to whom they sometimes allude), and make good use of opportunities to perform. I can still vividly recall the pleasure of hearing Muta read at the Creative Arts Centre at the University of the West Indies in the early 1970s. He more than holds his own in the company of other skilled performers such as Mikey Smith and Oku Onuora (formerly Orlando Wong) with whom he has recently shared programmes. But though, like the others, he is on intimate terms with reggae lyrics and he sometimes does angry poems, Muta resists the label of "dub poet" as much as "protest poet": each, he feels, refers to only one aspect of his work.

Granted that many of Muta's poems are fully realized only in performance, some of them seem to me far more successful than others. My own favourite is "Nursery Rhyme Lament" which, I am told, is now discussed in some of our schools. In "Dan is the Man in the Van", the famous calypso by The Mighty Sparrow, British nursery rhymes taught in colonial schools are pilloried as absurdly irrelevant in that context; in Muta's "Nursery Rhyme Lament" they are distorted into local meaning, they are reworked as history into the patterns of harsh reality – water rates, light bills, overpopulation, meat shortages and so on. The poem (especially when performed) is very funny; and deadly serious in the criticism it implies. Another special favourite of mine is "Revolutionary Poets" – "revolutionary poets/ ave become entertainers" – with its multiple ironies, including some that surely touch that poem itself. If few of the other pieces in this volume seem as fully achieved as these, this is, after all, a collection of "the first poems" in which the voice of the young Mutabaruka speaks to and for a host of troubled young people.

Kingston, 1980

The Poems

PART ONE

1970–1971
Call Me No Poet or Nothing Like That 2
Look Again 4
Oneness 5
White Sound 6
Weh Me Belang? 8
To the Blackboy, Yesterday 9
Black Queen 10
Say: 11

1972–1973
Nursery Rhyme Lament 12
The Outcry 14
The Change 16
Song of a Warrior 17
The Lament of I, the Slave 18
I, the Slave 20
I, the Slave: Despondent 22
Drum Song 23
Two Poems on What I Can Write 24
The Beginning; the End? The Beginning 26

1974
Dabaddabuninna (They Beat Me) 27
Wailin 28

PART TWO

1970
Friends 33

1971–1972
Never Stopping to Know 34
Revive 35
Retrieve 36
Reconcile 37
Muta's Monologue 38
You and Yourself 40

1973
To the Fish that Passed By 41
Mortal Me 42

1975
Church I 44
Church II 45
Since Today 46
Fulfilment 47
The Priest and U 48
Four Walls and One Window 49

1976
Faces and Places 50
My Poem, Your Mind 51
The Wheel 52

1978–1979
Metamorphosis 53
God is a Schizophrenic 54
Revolutionary Poets 56

part one

Call Me No Poet or Nothin Like That

i shall not never
write for lovers or
dream makers
        lillies
and moon shine romance
                never
unless   they are   me
free
i have no time
there are police beatin
brothers for being themselves
runnin around in streets
                7 o'clock
what?

call me no poet
or nothin like that

poems are for lovers
and actors
poems are for joy
and laugh/ter

shakespeare/milton/chaucer
still drenchin the souls of black folks
tryin to integrate
in my life   your life
poems   poems   poems
and we're still shittin in pit toilets
…runnin up and down
whistlin… nothin
be wise and realize there must be no poets recitin,
                   recit —
about

snow
where?
jones town?
trench town?
poems cannot heal
feel
batons and bullets... and
die away poetry

call me no poet
or nothin like that

whores in new kingston
man with molotov
babies dyin
rastas wantin to be free
no poems no poems
please
poets get black... back
black poets m o v e
this is no time to be dramatic
about abortion/food shortage
tax increase   life
shake   speare   must   lay   dead
forever
no recitals
no recitin
no poems
no poems
                    p
                      l
                        e
                          a
                            s
                              e

Look Again

Brought from the west coast of Africa
Brought to the kingdom called Jamaica
They baptized us, called us negro
I suppose the people from China are amarillo
Put us in chains all day
makin us work; little food, no pay
we continued like this a long, long time
pushed around and treated like swine
Sometimes we were lashed in the streets
left there too   dead meat
figuring how to get away
we ran to the hills and there we did stay
sometimes we came down to fight
they could not stand it they had a right
Freeman was near (so we thought)
until some of our brainwashed brothers got caught
they led men against us
that is why we always fuss

Black people in the west
put your brains to the test
get together and start again
oneness black people is the aim
Freeman this time is near at hand
unite black people all make one
look to the east just once this time
Africa once more for peace of mind

4

Oneness

shoutin:
Africa!
Ethiopia!
trying to
recollect
singin
talkin
what we need is an
harambee (togetherness)
joinin self to self
men?
how can that be?
man?
more togetherness.
man
oneness.
God one man
heart to heart
shapin map of Africa
"nuh more piece-a-piece, yah.
sight up JAH"
man in man
men
more than one
man
one.
God.
one GOD
man.

White Sound

everytime i hear the sound
everytime i hear the sound
everytime i hear the sound
the sound that sounds like:
remember nigger remember
the sound that sounds like:
the whips on your back
the sound that sounds like:
the chains round your neck
the sound that sounds like:
who raped your progenitors
the sound that sounds like:
who practised genocide on your people
the sound that sounds like:
who divided your race
stole your culture
the sound that sounds like:
infiltrated your land
corrupted your soil
the sound that sounds like:
planted the seeds of inferiority in your minds
kept down your progress
the sound that sounds like:
who built nations from nigger sweat nigger gold
the sound that sounds like:
remember nigger remember
you're no ethiopian
you're a negro
i named you a negro
the sound that sounds like:
remember nigger remember
you're no african
you're a negro
i named you a negro
the sound that sounds like:

SLAVE: BLACK SLAVE
BOSS: WHITE BOSS
GOOD: WHITE GOOD
BAD: BLACK BAD
everytime i hear the sound
everytime i hear the sound
everytime i hear the sound
the sound that sounds like
the sound that is not my name

Weh Mi Belang?

negro?
nigga?
west indian?
den a which country I belang?
chinese — china
indian — india
european — europe
negro?
nigga?
west indian?
den a which country i belang
negro — black
but negroland no
nigga — stupid but stupidland no
west yes but i nuh indian
den a which country i belang?

i affi guh trace
my original place
try fi fine out
wha mi is all about
a come yah fram de east
dat i know
an in de east
there is no negro
nigga?
dat i cyaa figga
west indian?
a which country i belang?

wait

a rememba a land
weh man ack like man
dem use fi call wi
NIGERIAN
GHANIAN
ETHIOPIAN

To the Blackboy Yesterday

Yesterday you saw yourself
as black as hell in sin

Yesterday you went to them to
compromise

Yesterday you hated your black sister
because she did not play with him

Yesterday you lied to your mommy
about not loving her

Yesterday you read a book and hated God
for letting you be born with black all over you

Yesterday you helped your sister to use
the hot comb
because you believed she wasn't as beautiful
as the girl in the book

Yesterday you wet yourself
because you wanted to lie with the
girl in the book

Yesterday you sold a brother
because he stole to survive

Yesterday you fought in wars
to keep peace in the world

Yesterday you were dead, blackboy

Yesterday is gone
                        today
blackboy

Black Queen

I see her.
I know her:
God's gift to man.
Fair and pleasant she stands
with her features projecting modesty,
her soul manifesting Godliness.
I await her call;
her lips to speak,
to touch my thoughts.
She speaks everlasting words,
her breath like the scent of cherries.
Speak now,
Queen of love.

    She loves God.
    She praises God;
    He made her
    of nothing that can be found on this earth.

      She is mesmerised by God:
      God's perfect creation.

I await her touch;
her touch awakens me from phantasms.
I feel my heart accelerating,
her touch a souvenir in my heart.

I see her, proud,
proud of her
blackness,
proud of her
blackman.
I see her, a black queen,
the First Queen,
Queen of queens.

Say:

(for Odun)

when you remember home
say: *ETHIOPIA*
when you remember slaves
say: *BLACK*
when you shout revolution
say: *FREEMAN*
when you shout babylon
say: *DEATH*
when you speak of education
say: *GET IT*
when you speak of unity
say: *WADADA*
when you speak of God
say: *MAN*
when you see culture
say: *RELATIVE TO...*
when you read all this
say: *MADNESSSSSS*
when you think like i
say: *RASTAFARI*

Nursery Rhyme Lament

first time
jack & jill
used to run up de hill everyday
now dem get pipe… an
water rate increase

everyday dem woulda
reincarnate humpty dumpty
fi fall off de wall

little bwoy blue
who loved to blow im horn
to de sheep in de meadow: little bwoy blue
grow up now… an
de sheep dem get curried
in a little cold suppa shop down de street

yu rememba when man was a ponder fi guh moon?
yet dem did ave de cat
fi play fiddle
so dat de cow coulda jump over it
every full moon… an
lite bill increase

den dere was de ol woman
who neva went to nuh fambly plannin clinic
she used to live someweh dung
back-o-wall inna one lef-foot shoe
back-o-wall in fashion now… an
she move

jack sprat… ah, yes, jack sprat
who couldn't stand fat; im start eat it now… but
im son a vegetarian… cause
meat scarce

little bo-peep who lost ar sheep… went out
to look fi dem
an find instead a politician… an
is now livin in beverly hills

mary
(yu know ar… she had a white lamb)
well, she saw bo-peep
an decide she woulda give ar lamb
to cinderella godmother fi
change im colour to black
before midday… an
society grow

little jack
rememba im?
im use fi siddung a de corna
a king st. & barry st.
de adda day im put im thumb
inna im mout… an
vomit… while
tom tom was stealin a woman wig
im fall inna jack vomit… an
bruk im friggin neck

tom tom fada, de pied piper
turn pro now… an
stop blow to rats
but realize seh
nuh rat neva falla im dung de rivva… an
im dead cause de clock strike 1:30… an
nuh mouse neva run down
                              tic   toc   tic
first time
man use fi love dem
but dis is not de time fi dem… cause
dem deh days done

…an wi write….

The Outcry

to walk the streets paved with blood
$$\text{mud}$$
mixed with sweat and tears
$$\text{years}$$
of dreams to materialize
$$\text{wise}$$
man
$$\text{seekin new plan}$$
$$\text{upsettin}$$
babylon.
gone above babylon infinity
new martyrs found 'mong so-called madness
$$\text{of the city}$$
$$\text{pity}$$
babylon can't see
$$\text{free}$$
$$\text{I}$$

Ras Tafari

herbs smell
$$\text{tell}$$
linkin man
to become one
why cry?
bring down from sky
$$\text{gods to die}$$
big samfie: lie
they talk of cultures
$$\text{vultures}$$
takin to turn
$$\text{yearn}$$
for truths
$$\text{roots}$$
look cute
$$\text{on youths}$$

comin back to wash
                            must crash
                                    now
how?
educate
        to emancipate
talk of freedom
                         some...
will come.
togetherness
                yes
leave west
           east best
unite and fight
                    sight
JAH light... it right
                                 mighty might

The Change

Yesterday
God was
white.
Good was white,
so
white was right.

Yesterday
evil was
black
so
i took stock.
today,
I changed.

Song of a Warrior

When will this war end
When will this war end
When will I return to my village again?

When will this war end
When will this war end
When will I call my enemies
friend?

The Lament of I, the Slave

a siddung ya fram
mawnin
waitin pon de ship
a lookin cross
de horizon
tryin fi rememba
a which direction
it was

it seem as if
mi waitin will guh
in vain
oh
what pain
how lang, O Lawd?

how lang
before a si mi mada
an fada again?
sometime
when a rememba
mi heart sink in sadness
how lang, O Lawd?
how lang?

a betta mek-kase an guh up now
yu soon ear massa a call
de ada day im call
an mi neva ear
de man… tie me dung pon de dutty
an...

O Lawd
why yu mek mi suffa so?

a si de ship!
Lawd gad... yu ansa mi praya!
bu-bu-buh but...
a wha dis mi si?
O Lawd...!
anada ship wid
more
a
mi

I, the Slave

Freeman, freeman
I sang songs
of freeman.

My mother
        chained to me
chained to them
I cried
     I cried
cried because they took my brother
my brother
       still suckin
my mother's breast
my brother

was fed to the sea

I cried
     I cried
my mother they whipped
whipped her because
she cried
       about them whippin my father
she, the slave
       he, the slave.
Then I would arise
at sun-nearly-rise
workin away my life
no name
no name
I knew no name
I, the forgotten soul
whipped to live
whipped because I lived
whipped to
       death

Today, I sing songs
redemption songs
freein mother
                    freein father
I sing songs to be free
freein
I the slave
I, the slave....

I, the Slave: Despondent

I was brought here
to make
to make of this island…
a mother;
oh mother
          oh mother
I can remember your cuddling arms.
   now
   I must find new comforts;
   I remember your teachings
   of love,
   of life.
   now
   I hate living
   …and when I remember you, mother,
   I wonder.

It is now 19 years
since I came
to these shores.

Where are the comforts?
where is the love
and
livings?
where is
          mother?
mother
mother
oh mother
Where is mother…

Africaaaaaaaaa?

Drum Song

i speak
      you listen
i send messages above
                    your thoughts
i caress your soul
makin it elusive
i speak   you dance
you dance
          your   end   less
dance
awakenin the mystery of life
life not as you know it
life as you dream it
when   i speak
i speak of love
i speak enhancin words
reachin greatness
          end   less
ly
i speak also of deaths
deaths entanglin deaths
deaths that start livins
i enslave to set free
i breed
     among you i breed
              yourself
only you will know it
i speak to free you from your self.
yourself that was lost
          until
i spoke   i speak of
greater freeman   in the heights i go
           slow...
to pass my message
my message that will build
man
        one

Two Poems on What I Can Write

can i write poems
                about:
tall green grass
shadin the tough
earth,
                about:
dew drops on beautiful
spreadin lillies?

can i write
of lovers
            makin love
in parks
with moon shine caressin
their faces?
...of rainbow-coloured birds
singin their nature songs
in tall lush trees?

all of this i can write.

                but now,
                i write....

i write of tall trees
shadin black skins
                    from
hot death
of:
guns   and
bombs
hidden under spreadin white sheets

i write
of people
bein shot down in parks
with blood washin their faces
…of negroes and
                coloureds
shoutin their freedom songs
in tall anti-freedom
buildins
                all this i write.

The Beginning; the End? The Beginning

it was in Eden i saw you first
there we shared our love and
listened to the rhythm of the gentle breeze
emulating God's love songs;
we knew ourself then.

our bodies glittered with rays of life
skins black as the first light that
created   we knew all things
all things were we
out of the earth we were moulded
through God's breath we lived:
Solomons/Aesops/Akhnatons/Lokmans/
Cleopatras/Shebas/Zenobias
we were gods to be worshipped by mortals
but then we knew ourselves.

again we await
that immortal life,
lost among this life of deaths
drained of our love

we seek

we seek the garden of Eden
there we left our love
and our God

ETHIOPIA...!

Dabaddabuninna (They Beat Me)

Never forgetting memories
of yesterday's agonies
still lingering in my
                              physicalness,
bodies drained of their blood,
thunder sounds of whips
cracking against black flesh —
I piss/I shit
"DABADDABUNINNA!"

Bleed/bleed/bleeding
flesh seperation
lips held together
salt in blood
agony cry
souls   dying;
        death/death/death
              calling
"DABADDABUNINNA!"

Crying away love
creating new evils;
I think like the whip
I move like the whip
I piss
        in tears   and
blood;
I hate the whip
and those who use it.

Never will I stop crying
yesterday's memories will
always linger

I see it today in my
black flesh
DABADDABUNINNA

Wailin

juke box play
...an "stir it up"
in de ghetto
yout man
            "run fi cova"
hot
hot
        hotter
"curfew" in a trench town
gun a blaze:
                crack
"trench town rock"

juke box playin
...an wi sayin
"long time wi nuh ave nuh nice time"
yout man
            watch yu step
mek-kase   stop
                    "screwface"
"lively up yuself"
an "come reason now"
yout man
            watch yu ways
"simma down"
                stop frown

play music
play in a "mellow mood"
                music is food
in de ghetto
yout man
            spread out
            stop bungle
inna "concrete jungle"
            watch it

mutabaruka

in de ghetto
hot
   ...hippies smokin pot?
wha dat?
yout man
       throw wey de
molotov bomb
oppressa-man
         man vex
who yu gwine shoot nex?
hey you big tree
        "small axe"
ready

part two

Friends

all my friends are
white
nearly white
or brown skinned

all my friends are
capitalist
imperialist
fascist
racist
murderers and thieves

all my friends are
negroes
niggers
negrophiles

all my friends are
church folks
godly people
prayin to sky god

all my friends are
livin dead
tryin to escape
from themselves

Never Stoppin to Know

Never stoppin to know
i place my mind on things i can see
things i can create without
motivatin my true ability
idolisin my creations   i think on....

but what have i created?
                              not life
i've created a thinkin myth
my true self is not in my thinkin
thinkin to satisfy my complacency
never stoppin to know

i need to know myself
not myself that i can see
myself that is inaccessible
myself from the alpha
i manifested my creations in many ways
yet not creatin problems for myself
the thinkin i is theoretical
the man spiritual is above all
the man thinkin is "me"
thinkin on the care of my body
of my worldly possessions
never stoppin to know
that all worldly
things
must
go

Revive

Burnin bright
burnin bright
oil lamp burnin.
Drum chants
praises to...
mind reunion,
awakenin.
cry for the livin
or
cry for life?
Escapin from the
much loved day
now revealed in
blackenin night.
Death is never
dead are livin,
takin part
in a
despised art

Retrieve

Hear the drum beat
echoin through the trees
the bonfire
blazin endlessly
so they dance
KUMINA/KUMINA
tramplin, tremblin
the ground vibrates.
Chantin praises to
their gods
no danger seems to exist.
For far away
a distant past has revealed
itself to them
now they are aware
the present past has elapsed.

So they dance, from dusk till dawn
knowin now that this was it
and now will be
perpetual.

Reconcile

Today it was
I looked out to the sea
and saw my life
reaching the horizon;
I called... but was not heard.
The waves
I remember the waves
God I am lost
          find me
             reach me
teach me   let me look to myself again.
Then comes the solitude
and I wait   wait?
I await the answer to set me free
from this... this unblessed shore
I am domiciled   help me
I am crying   comfort me.

How peaceful it would have been
if I was left to be alone with myself.
...I was with God
The God.
The horizon; I   move
and it stretches
further and further...
              STOP!
and let me touch you

let me feel you and realize myself,
myself embedded on these shores
I am domiciled   help me
I am crying   comfort me
I am lost to God
God the Creator
God the Me
God the God.

Muta's Monologue

I got home late last night,
conscious of the night
conscious of the fright
mind lost in the loneliness of youth
I say, why am I searching the night?
now I must start again, believe me, I must,
I say, where should I go tonight?
it would be a pleasure to sit quietly and...
now I should remember.
Fuck it all why should I care
sorrow is sorrow,
death is death,
        life is for living
                now.
In my heart there has been a melody
                gone.
Gone to stay, gone yesterday, gone forever;
striking fast, slowly and surely, never returning.
Bury the thoughts, crash them set them to death.

Out of the night's darkness comes unlimited
imagining
reacting impulsively, not brave enough to face
this reality;
time to forget, time to cast this night and its
melancholy loneliness away.
The darkness is solid, it rests hard against
my thoughts
        of life
everlasting life I'll have to find, or be dead now
                sickening.
Vain is the me that seekest after death, once
                dead
always serene
I fearing? fearing not the light nor the darkness
                the end is nigh.

Now I must go leaving the night to rest,
leaving the dead to answer to God,
leaving the night to turn day
                                        ending....

You and Yourself

You
pleased with yourself
for freein yourself
havin seen yourself
in a world by yourself
not knowin yourself
to question yourself
about yourself
that enslaves
You

To the Fish that Passed by

Today i stepped into your world
"I'm sorry if i did wrong"
How quiet it must have been before i came
                                        now
The water is dirty
i came to wash away my troubles
"I'm sorry if i washed long"
i a man
tried to imprison you
but then
i realized
"I'm sorry i stifled you"
at that moment
i wondered
could i be free
free as you
my heart sank in sadness
how i envied you

today i stepped into your world
"I'm sorry if i did wrong"

Mortal Me

here i dwell a mortal
perverted by veil of evil red
stained with lewd impressions
of he who bears the scythe:
encases mortals heart once unstained
depicts the fungi-sin
which erodes life within,
created by mortals of ancient lore
this evil red i do abhor
for 'tis the symbol... death.

here i dwell like all the rest
i too represent a livin death
my soul belies... aloft.

ancient ones spake of He
a heart of livin fire
an aura 'round His head
saviour of souls of men
He came
was crucified for mortal souls...
but the evil red still stands
omnipresent in the hearts of every man.

here i dwell a mortal
illusions all around
premonitions occur:
discard the veil of evil red
that binds one to the livin dead.

omnipotent is HE
that came into my heart
transgressions He cleansed from i
mortal free
immortal   i
true life immortal knew
HIS CREATION
and HE THE CREATOR... too.

Church I

Bells ringin
no church today
corpses are being taken to the house
                                of the livin
no church for me
preacher standin on his pulpit
pulpin out your mind
pervertin...
crucifyin u
choir echoin echoin

                                dreams unreal
spirits in the sky;
                                on earth too

marble statues
                        rapin your soul
tellin u to die again
images carve out your life
                        collection time.
money for the preacher
                                the teacher-god
sellin your soul to who?
taste of wine
                        blood of the people
remindin u of your little pub next door

sunday mornin goin now
u shall come again
u have just saved yourself — again
u have just repented your week's sins — again
now the bells ring once more
the corpses are being led away
                                        to the
                                                grave....

Church II

Void of people
silent still
a vast dome of worship
sparklin pews of wood
cold altars of marble
crosses there crosses here
big crosses   little crosses
all depictin death

large whistles
blown by hands
sad bewailin sounds
all depictin death
in the house of the livin
                              dead

Since Today

it is now dusk —
since today
i have
washed my face
i have
washed my hands
i have
washed my feet
since today
i have bathed my skin
                              twice

since today
i have washed away much dirt
but now
dusk is takin away the day
this man
lookin in the mirror
still sees dirt
                    because he is
                              earth

Fulfilment

the day is dark   now
i remember the night.
no birds.
standin still over there is a tree
                          no leaves
the earth breeds
          and life appears... worms

saviours of the time
seers of the past
behold man is lost
caught in webs
              untold agonies
driftin away
        in deserts of gloom
Christ the saviour
mocked by man
pierced by man
Christ the life in man

behold man is lost
mockin himself to death
callin   but he is not heard

the night shall not come
the day is dark enough
and now you must take away the shackles
the earth still breeds
             and life must appear
                in the
               resurrection

The Priest and U

sunday
an u sit there again
                    listenin
listenin to the message of
god or maybe....

sittin there doin nothin
your soul is bein saved again

watchin u watchin him
drinkin wine with him
the bench is gettin hot
it will soon be done
he turns to u
"Deus vobiscum"
now u are ready
the task is done

he has used your mind
to make love
with the
dead

Four Walls and One Window

I came here yesterday
sick
dying
Not sure of who
or what led me
to return
Sprawling on the bed
face looking up
up to the ceiling
trying to remember
trying to find an answer
to this...
tracing the ceiling
where it meets the wall
cobweb all over
leaking too
I had wondered
if I'd return
been weeks
months probably
I had everything
where I was
Oh God
why?
Why should I?
I've got to find the answer
today
tomorrow
I will be dead
Somehow, somewhere it's there
but now
I cannot think
this room
Four walls
and
one window

Faces and Places

Earth
faces and places
impressions of the mind;
hotter than the hottest fire
               keep calm
                   it's me.
Earth
playing with your body
getting older than you...
faces and places...
traces of madness
             maybe sadness.
Castrate your thoughts
better to have none —
faces and places
this could be you
moving like a ship
              that is battered by the waves
no sweat
       at least not yet
I AM THE CAPTAIN OF YOUR MIND
LAND, AHOY!
but this is earth
of course it is — where else could this be
you are trying to play games with me
          play on
               oh mortals of the dirt
play on — net yourself
remember I am your captain speaking.
Faces and places
this is earth... this is earth... come in — over
hello... hello... hell low
            earth

Another child is born
another fool is dead
oh fools of the earth
encasing yourself in nothing
faces and places

My Poem Your Mind

here i am sittin here
writin you my poem
seein your mind tryin to reach

                    mine

in my poem
you see many things
includin nothing

in your mind
i see you
havin an orgasm

                tryin to put my poem together
here i sit waitin
for you to realize
to understand
that i can write nothin
for you to think on

there is everything
already in my poem
that is in your

             mind....

The Wheel

(for Jennifer and Pauline)

and when you stop
the world
and you that dwell in it
will still be here
to face

the another of
YOU

Metamorphosis

caterpillar crawlin
                    crawlin
turnin...
watch yourself
                    changin
caterpillar...   here
                    movin slowly
surely
watch yourself
                    changin
                    changin
caterpillar
changin
                    changin
to
        butterfly
watch yourself...
                    watch
your
self

beautiful

        butterfly....

God is a Schizophrenic

talkin this
talkin that
everyone tryin to find
where its at
me   u
u   me
all of us
tryin to be free
now the clock says its time
    tic   toc   tic
god is a schizophrenic

today u do this
tomorrow u do that
god   and   devil
both in u
everything been done
come from who?
mornin and night
woman and man
rich and poor
tryin to be one
wonderin what is sin
time steps in
    tic   toc   tic
god is a schizophrenic

check this out
without a doubt
today things are bad
today u are happy
tomorrow u are sad
goin through many changes
in a very short time
poverty is still linked with crime
now the clock
moves once again
who's to answer
who's to blame
    tic   toc   tic
god is a schizophrenic

now all u religious people out there
i know u might not like what u hear
god in the sky
come down to die
god in the sky
a universal lie
u out there
sayin this
sayin that
still don't know
where it's at
rich and poor
the clock moves again
    tic   toc   tic
god is a schizophrenic

Revolutionary Poets

revolutionary poets
ave become entertainers
babblin out angry words
about
                    ghetto yout
bein shot down
guns an bombs
                    yes
revolutionary words bein
digested with
                    bubble gums
                    popcorn an
                    ice cream
in   tall   inter   conti   nental
                                    buildins

revolutionary poets
ave become entertainers
oppressors recitin about   oppressors
oppressin   the   oppressors
                            where are the oppressed?

revolutionary poets
ave become entertainers
sippin coffee an tea
explainin what it's like
to be   down   twn
aroun   twn
up   twn   dancin   to
                    bee   gees
gettin night fever
while the
salvation army is still leadin the
                            revolution

mutabaruka

revolutionary poets
ave become entertainers
revoltin against change
thats takin place
in their heads while old ladies an others
are shot down dead
                             cant write about that

yes revolutionary poets
ave all gone to the
creative arts centre
to watch
the sufferin
of the people
bein dram   at   ized by the
oppressors
                  in their
                      revolutionary
                              poems